# The BESTSELLING BOOK FORMULA

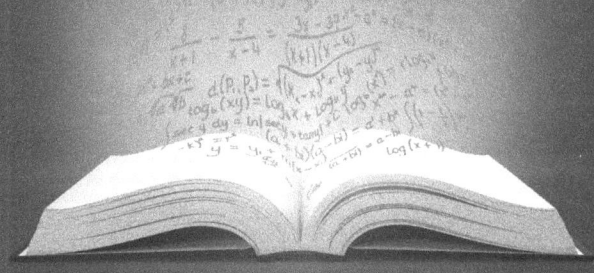

**WRITE A BOOK THAT WILL MAKE YOU A FORTUNE**

# HONORÉE CORDER

AUTHOR, *YOU MUST WRITE A BOOK*

# THE
# BESTSELLING BOOK
# FORMULA

WRITE A BOOK THAT
MAKES YOU A FORTUNE

# HONORÉE CORDER

Copyright 2023 © Honorée Enterprises Publishing, LLC

All rights reserved. No part of this book may be reproduced or transmitted in any form or by any means, electronic or mechanical, including photocopying, recording, or by any information storage and retrieval system without written permission of the publisher, except for the inclusion of brief quotations in a review.

Designed by Dino Marino, www.dinomarino.com.

Paperback ISBN: 978-1-947665-20-0

Digital ISBN: 978-1-947665-21-7

# ALSO BY HONORÉE CORDER

## THE *YOU MUST* BOOK BUSINESS SERIES

- *I Must Write My Book:*
  *The Companion Workbook to You Must Write a Book*
- *You Must Market Your Book:*
  *Increase Your Impact, Sell More Books, and Make More Money*
- *I Must Market My Book:*
  *The Companion Workbook to You Must Market Your Book*
- *You Must Monetize Your Book (September 2023)*
- *I Must Monetize My Book (September 2023)*

## OTHER BOOKS & SERIES

- *Business Dating: Applying Relationship Rules*
  *in Business for Ultimate Success*
- *Tall Order: Organize Your Life*
  *and Double Your Success in Half the Time*
- *Vision to Reality: How Short Term Massive Action*
  *Equals Long Term Maximum Results*
- *The Divorced Phoenix: Rising from the Ashes*
  *of a Broken Marriage*
- *If Divorce is a Game, These are the Rules:*
  *8 Rules for Thriving Before, During and After Divorce*
- The *Like a Boss* Book Series
- The *Miracle Morning* Book Series
- The *Prosperity for Writers* Book Series
- The *Successful Single Mom* Book Series

# SPECIAL INVITATION

I'd like to personally invite you to join the Prosperous Writer Mastermind Facebook Group: Facebook.com/groups/ProsperityforWriters. In this positive group, you'll find support, motivation, resources, and help.

> Be sure to sign-up for instant access to all of the resources I include in this book:
>
> HonoreeCorder.com/Formula

# **TABLE OF CONTENTS**

Introduction ........................................................i

**CHAPTER ONE**
The Bestselling Book Formula ......................... 1

**CHAPTER TWO**
Key #1: Easy to Read ....................................... 5

**CHAPTER THREE**
Key #2: Easy to Remember ............................ 15

**CHAPTER FOUR**
Key #3: Easy to Do ........................................ 28

**CHAPTER FIVE**
Key #4: Easy to Share..................................... 39

**CHAPTER SIX**
Not too Long, Not too Short,
Juuuust Right!................................................ 49

**CHAPTER SEVEN**
Books that Pass The Bestselling Book Formula Test ......................................... 53

**CHAPTER EIGHT**
Put the Bestselling Book Formula to Work in Your Book .................................. 66

Author's Notes .............................................. 80

Action Guide ................................................ 84

Bestselling Book Formula Mini-Course ......... 85

Book Recommendations .............................. 86

Would You Kindly Review This Book? .......... 87

Gratitude ..................................................... 88

Who is Honorée Corder? ............................... 90

# **INTRODUCTION**

Dear Reader,

I'm so glad you're here! I was excited to write this book because I want every book to be truly and wildly successful over a long period of time. I discovered this formula "by accident on purpose." I think if it were known by authors before they began writing, it could truly help them write a bestselling book.

I sure wish I'd known it back when I started writing!

I stumbled upon this formula when I started analyzing why some books had staying power, which also meant they had earning power.

I studied dozens of books, and while some had other factors that influenced their staying power, the four I identified were present in every single book. I was intrigued, to say the least.

The books I chose had been consistently selling for years (some for decades), and while millions of others have come and gone, they are still around ... selling, selling, selling. And being read, acted upon, and shared.

Those books, which I share in Chapter Seven, all had these four elements in common: the book's title, premise, and/or formula were easy to *read, remember, do,* and *share.* I share these elements as the keys to unlocking the golden door of success for your book.

I started looking at every book through this formula, and sure enough, the ones that make an impact and an income all shared these four elements, which when combined, made book-selling magic!

Why? I believe this because at the very top of the list of ways people discover a book is "personal recommendation."

The books I reviewed—every single one—and others I've discovered since that initial study, all meet these criteria. And while I'm primarily focused on nonfiction, there are many fiction authors and titles that meet these criteria as well.

Which is why, when you know this formula, you can use it while you are *crafting* your book. You won't have to hope your book will be successful; you can almost ensure it. Your book can be a bestselling book!

The formula and how you apply it to your book—that's the premise of this short book.

*However*. The title of this book is a tad misleading. Allow me to clarify one major point before we get into the formula and how you can apply it to your book.

The term *bestseller* needs clarification.

These days, I see almost everyone posting something like this:

- In just eight hours, my book was a #1 bestseller on Amazon!
- My book is #1 on Amazon!

What they should say is:

- *In just eight hours, my book was a #1 bestseller* in an obscure category *on Amazon,* which really means I sold five copies to my mother. In one hour.

- *My book is #1* in the kitten legwarmer category, even though my book's topic is Leadership *on Amazon*. And I've sold 22 copies to my coaching clients and three to my Aunt Ethel. In one hour.

**Being a true bestselling book and hitting #1 on Amazon actually means being #1 overall in the Amazon store.** But since Amazon has over sixteen thousand categories, some folks conveniently choose to ignore reality and claim their book is #1. Members of the general public just go, "Wow! #1! That's amazing! Congratulations!"

They don't know they've been hoodwinked. They don't know that Prada bag is actually a knock-off purchased for $20 in Chinatown. *They think #1 is #1.*

Funnily enough, the actual authors who hit #1 on Amazon almost never post about it. They are too busy doing something else. I digress.

These same "#1" authors have a book that ranks #1, yes, but it isn't truly bestselling.

The truth is their book hit #1 in a sub-category on Amazon, and it is probably only #1 for a few hours or a few days. Did you know the category rankings are updated *hourly?* I've legit seen a book rank #1 for one hour, then the next hour it was

#16, then a few days later it wasn't ranked in any category at all (the book has to at least be in the top 100 of a category to rank).

So, if a book isn't truly bestselling, there's no possible way it is best *earning*.

Which is what I know every author truly wants: a bestselling book that is also a best earning book. This means the book is continuously selling (hour over hour, month over month, year over year), making the author money. Most likely, it ranks high in a few sub-categories and is *nowhere near the actual #1 spot on Amazon.*

Which is totally cool in my world; I love having books that sell continuously and rank in sub-categories, year over year. I can pay my bills with that!

In my publishing course, Publishing Ph.D., I share the contents of this book as a "bonus for a bestseller." I share the distinction between **bestseller** and **best earner:**

A bestselling book can sell just a few copies in one hour and rank very high in a few categories, but it is, in reality, not really what anyone would consider bestselling.

*A best earning book is a book that sells continuously, over time, and earns the author money both in royalties as well as in new business.*

Not all bestselling books are best earning books, but all best earning books are bestsellers.

Now that you're clear on the difference, you probably want a best earning book, amiright? (I thought so.) Then let's get this party started. Please turn the page.

CHAPTER ONE

# **THE BESTSELLING BOOK FORMULA**

The Bestselling Book Formula is simple, so simple, that once you understand it, you'll be able to apply it to your book long before you publish. In fact, you can apply it to your book's outline, even before you begin writing.

You'll be able to see it in perennial sellers, books that have staying power. You'll also see how the author missed the mark in others.

And, if you've published before, you might have a little insight into why your book didn't do as well as you would have liked. *For a little about what to do if you've already published and wish you'd had this information sooner, I share my thoughts in my Author Notes at the end of this book.*

For the remainder of this book (and forevermore), keep in mind when I say bestselling or bestseller, what I really mean is best earning or best earner. Cool? Good.

If you want your book to be a true bestselling book, an everlasting seller, there are i's to dot and t's to cross, and I'm sharing them with this formula. Now please keep in mind there are other boxes to check (quality is one of them, and having a solid marketing plan is another), but I'm not including them in this short book. I have other books on these topics, and there is also plenty of information you can find on every aspect of writing, marketing, and publishing books. (I've included a list in the back of this book.)

*This* book has one purpose and one purpose only: to give you a list and breakdown of the common elements I've discovered most bestselling books contain so you can apply it to your future books to give them the best chance of massive success.

To help make it easy (or at least easier), I've created a *test*, The Bestselling Book Formula Test, which I use to evaluate books. You can get your own test in the book's bonuses at [HonoreeCorder.com/Formula](HonoreeCorder.com/Formula)

First, let me share the Formula, then the Test.

## THE BESTSELLING BOOK FORMULA

The Bestselling Book Formula consists of four elements or *keys*, and they are: *read, remember, do,* and *share*. What that means is that the book's title, premise, and/or the formula contained within it are easy to:

1. *read,*
2. *remember,*
3. *do*, and
4. *share.*

Also, a bestselling book has a ten or more-year shelf-life because it meets the highest quality standard. Again, not what I'm talking about in this book—but without meeting at least basic quality standards, your otherwise golden goose of a book will languish in obscurity.

## THE BESTSELLING BOOK FORMULA TEST

I think of the Test as a set of filters. Each question has a yes or no answer:

1. Is the book easy to read?
2. Is the book's title or formula easy to remember?
3. Is what the book teaches easy to do?
4. Is the book's title or formula easy to share?

By virtue of setting a fine example, I've made this book, *The Bestselling Book Formula,* in and of itself, easy to read, remember, do, and share.

Give it a try: without looking, what's the title of this book? What are the four elements?

To be fair, you don't have to look far to find them. Also, you're not at the end of the book yet so my work is not done! *smile*

I'm going to do my best to teach this to you in simple, easy to read, remember, do, and share ways. When you know it, and you know how to apply it, you'll never forget it, *and* you'll benefit greatly from it—and that's what I'm here to teach you.

Let's dive in!

CHAPTER TWO

# KEY #1: EASY TO READ

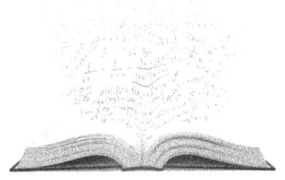

Almost every bestselling book is easy to read.

Before you start throwing fancy book titles around, I'm not talking about *literature* or required reading to obtain advanced degrees.

The books I analyzed on the way to discovering this formula are nonfiction, specifically in the self-help, personal development, or business development space. In fact, they are the books you most likely will have heard of, or when you look them up, you will wonder why you hadn't already.

Mostly this is because they have hundreds, if not thousands, of reviews, have been around for several years, and are still selling well.

According to The Literacy Project the average American reads at a 7$^{th}$ to 8$^{th}$ grade level (and sadly, we are well below the overall world's average).

*"This is too easy to read."*

~Nobody ever

What I'm talking about is *readability*: the state of being read and understood.

Readability is extremely important. In fact, no one wants to read *at* their level; they prefer to read at a level below their capacity. *Nobody* wants it to be harder. Even highly literate, highly educated audiences perform better with more readable content.

I have a ton of respect for education, and I do love a ten-dollar word. *However.*

When I'm reading, I don't love it when I have to stop and look up a word. Your readers won't either. Too many "I don't know what that means," and they'll put the book down and pick up another one. You've lost them and failed the first question of the test.

We don't want that, right? Right!

I want your book to be successful, *and* I don't want you to change who you are—I simply want your book to reach as wide an audience as humanly possible. That means you've got to use the structure and vocabulary your readers will be able to grasp; *easily*.

What does this mean exactly? I'm glad you asked because I've given it a lot of thought (and have done some research).

It turns out being *easy to read* is a bit more nuanced than you might first think. And before you dismiss this as, "these people aren't my audience," hold the phone there, Sparky! As I mentioned, *no one* wants to read content they don't easily grasp in a reasonable amount of time, leaving them unsatisfied.

I mean, they picked up your book for at least one reason. In fact, they might have more than one reason.

People read nonfiction books because they:

- Want to avoid pain and suffering, or
- gain pleasure,
- or both.

If your book is above their reading level and they just can't get through it, they won't be happy. As it turns out, neither will you! They will also do two things that are a huge bummer: they won't finish your book, and they certainly won't recommend it.

I would be remiss if I didn't mention that your book's contents need to be *special, fantastic,* and *helpful,* and not *useless* or *silly.* You won't have a bestselling book if your content is easily found on Google (people buy books *en masse* because the information is exclusive). It also won't be a bestselling book if you write on a topic that doesn't make sense (you won't sell a ton of books about "painting a cat" or "knitting kitten legwarmers").

## HELP YOUR READER WIN

The antidote to this is to have a clear understanding of what makes a book *easy to read.* After all, you want your readers to feel like they've won—like their time has been well spent—they've gotten value and can benefit from what they've read. I've discovered there are three desired reader outcomes to consider as you write:

***Understanding.*** What you write should be *easily* understood by the reader. A confused mind says, "Nope!" This same mind then decides they don't want to finish reading your book. The first positive is when a reader understands what they've read.

***Time.*** Simple to read text increases speed and decreases reading time. Have you ever said, "The text in that book was dense, and I had a hard time getting through it?" Me, too. Did you power through? Probably not, or only when you had to. Me, too, again. And I certainly did not enjoy it! A quick read helps your reader feel successful, which leads to …

***Satisfaction***. When your reader understands what you've written, and they can read it in record time, their satisfaction rate goes up. You know what else goes up? Their likelihood to feel good about themselves and your book. This is important for them to carry out the rest of The Bestselling Book Formula.

What's a writer to do? I've got you covered.

## MAKE YOUR WRITING EASY TO READ

***Just write.*** Go ahead and write in your voice with your normal word choices. I don't want to risk curbing your creative juices.

When you're writing your first draft, just write. Sometimes it's hard enough to find the intersection of flow, time, and writing without worrying about your eventual reader's ability to read and understand your writing.

Please just get the words out of your head and onto the page. Write with abandon! There will be plenty of time to review and revise with these next two pieces of advice in mind:

**Short sentences win.** Are you prone to extra-long sentences? I'm guilty of this writing "sin" as well.

Not one of my first (or second) drafts has passed muster without my editor suggesting I divide some of my long sentences into shorter ones.

It turns out my editors (all of them) have had a method to their madness—or shall I say picky-ness?

There's almost a one-to-one relationship between sentence length and comprehension. The shorter the sentence, the higher the comprehension. Use eight words or less; readers understand one hundred percent. Use fourteen words or less; readers understand about ninety percent. The more words, including prepositions and conjunctions, the less readers understand.

Lack of understanding equates to lack of reading. Lack of reading means lack of finishing. Lack of finishing means no bestseller for you.

I love to focus on the positive, so allow me to flip this. Increased understanding increases reading. Increased reading means more readers will finish your book. Increased readership can equal bestseller status for you and your book! Better, right?

But wait, there's more!

**Short words also win.** Why say *employment* when *jobs* will do? Turns out, there's a solid reason for shorter word choices.

Longer words are harder to read, and vocabulary is a top predictor of difficulty. Short, simple words boost one's ability to read and comprehend.

I know you don't want to sound stuffy or arrogant, nor do you want to come across as dishonest.

Familiar and common words are easy to understand, and one-syllable words and word familiarity increase clarity. They also position you as someone who is both knowledgeable and approachable.

One of the biggest ideas in the history of the United States was expressed in the Gettysburg Address. Of the 235 words Lincoln used in the Gettysburg Address (that's fewer than the number on the back of a potato chip package today), 174 of them have only one syllable.

*We can* express big ideas with small words. In fact, short words express ideas faster and to more people than long words.

Lest you think that you are dumbing down your years of education and eliminating some ten-dollar words you love (I'm a fan of some, too), there's no cause for concern. I believe a truly intelligent person is able to take complex information and simplify it so anyone can understand it.

You're a truly intelligent person. You're going to combine your education, experience, knowledge, and expertise and put it in an easy-to-read format, including, and when possible (unlike this one), short sentences with short words. Your reader can then easily read it, and hopefully love it.

## YOU'RE NOT ALONE IN THIS PROCESS

In addition to your own careful review, you'll be able to rely on your editorial team to help you. When working with your editors and proofreader, ask them specifically to point out when you use longer sentences. They can also identify needlessly long words.

*Note:* Yes, I did use Thesaurus.com almost a dozen times in this chapter to double check my word choices. I wanted to see if there was a shorter substitute for "unnecessarily" and got four options: needlessly (which I used in the preceding paragraph), avoidably, optionally, and unessentially. I mention this because I've spent lots of time with the site during this chapter. I encourage you to remain calm and not overthink your word choices and sentence lengths.

I believe my point is made about writing in a way readers can read, digest, and use the contents of your book. Yet that's only one-quarter of the journey to a bestselling book.

Next, you need to craft your book in a way that helps the reader remember, against the odds. And the odds are many! So, let's continue; we definitely want to keep your message top of mind.

## ASPIRING BESTSELLING AUTHOR BOOK CLUB?

*If you're so inclined, gather up a gaggle of authors or aspiring authors and use this as a book club book. For your convenience, and to get the party started, I've included a few discussion questions at the end of each chapter, starting with this one.*

# CHAPTER TWO BOOK CLUB DISCUSSION QUESTIONS

1. Based on Key #1: *Easy to Read*, how does your book or WIP (work-in-process) stack up?

2. What ideas came to mind when reading this chapter?

3. How will adjusting your writing allow your reader to be more successful, more quickly?

4. Do you resist tailoring your content so it is digestible by your readers?

5. What is your biggest takeaway from this chapter?

CHAPTER THREE

# KEY #2: EASY TO REMEMBER

Some of you reading this book will have discovered my work through *The Miracle Morning* book series. At least three times a week, I'll have a conversation with someone, and they'll tell me just that.

*Almost.*

I did a podcast interview yesterday, and the host said, "I loved your work with *The Morning Miracle! I still do the SAVERS …*"

I just nod and smile, grateful that T*he Miracle Morning* is easy for people to remember (even if sometimes incorrectly) for two reasons. One of them we'll discuss in this chapter; the other, we'll cover more deeply in Chapter Four.

When writing your book, crafting your title, and/or creating a formula, using tools like acronyms or acrostics to help your reader recall your work is critical.

Key #2 is to have a hook, a phrase, a formula—any or all of these can ensure that in the right moment (the one when it comes time for your reader to recall your book or something about it)—*they can remember.*

With everything humans have to remember, including birthdays, wedding dates, social security numbers, passcodes and passwords, jargon, names, addresses, and the list goes on, handing them the ability to recall your work at will is not only helpful, it's critical.

I mean, it's a miracle we remember anything at all, isn't it?

Our brains are funny things. Sometimes they work better than the best computer; other times, they stall and crash, like an old, over-used laptop. Or is it just my brain that fails me, sometimes when I need it the most?

When was the last time you tried to share something—anything—and you simply *could not?* You paused. Took a moment. Apologized for not remembering it off the top of your head. Shook your head in disdain, all while feeling frustrated. You *knew it*, whatever *it* was, but it just wouldn't come to you in that moment.

You said, "It'll come to me later, and I'll tell you when it does." (But you didn't, did you?)

Then, later, it popped into your head. *Of course, that's the answer.* Then you got on with your day, the moment missed, and the intended share never happened.

In your case, you, the book author, your title, or formula, were left unshared.

By concentrating on making your book title, content, or formula (or all three) memorable, you'll boost the chances people will remember it just when you need them to the most—when it's time to share about it!

Oh, we're going to talk about the sharing a bit later. For now, let's ensure your readers can *remember* first.

## WHAT MAKES SOMETHING EASY TO REMEMBER?

I'm pretty sure you're with me, and you want readers to be able to remember you and your book. Most authors don't consider crafting their book title, contents, or formula with a focus on *memorability.* They—you—can do a lot to ensure it is worth remembering *and* easily recalled.

Because you're still working on your book—even if you're almost ready to publish—you can still spend some time making what could be micro-adjustments to strengthen your book. Here are some suggestions:

## CRISP

**Make it *crisp*, as in succinct or brief.** Hal Elrod, the author of *The Miracle Morning*, was brilliant in choosing his book's title. It meets the Formula's criteria for being memorable in a couple of ways.

First, it is short and sweet! Just as short sentences are helpful for readability, short book titles are useful when it comes to being memorable.

Think about when you could remember a book's concept, but not the author's name or the book's title. *Missed opportunity.*

Actually, it's a triple missed opportunity: the author, the sharing reader, and the possible reader.

*Oh no.*

Even when people flip *morning* and *miracle*, they've recalled the book's title (which you'll understand the importance of when we get to Chapter Six, "Easy to Share").

When designing your book title, brevity, *being brief,* is your BFF. There are several nonfiction titles that easily come to mind (ahem) because they are concise: *The 4-Hour Work Week, Go for No, Think & Grow Rich.* There are also fiction titles that immediately and always come to mind: *Pride & Prejudice*, *A Tree Grows in Brooklyn*, and more recently, *Verity*.

**CATCHY**

**Catchy is code for "it catches."** It catches in your brain and sticks like Gorilla Glue.

*The Miracle Morning* is also catchy. It is easy to remember because the word *miracle* is pleasant—I mean, who doesn't want a miracle? It is also memorable and becomes even more so when combined with the word *morning*. About fifty percent of people will say they aren't morning people. The title causes people to pause and consider the concept of having "a miracle morning." Combining miracle and morning together can, at least to some, create an immediate and thoughtful pause.

When choosing your book's title, err on the side of catchy. However, I caution you against being cute or clever beyond our previously discussed reader's reading level. Very simply, if you have to explain your book title, it isn't the right title (even if it is short and catchy).

One of my Publishing Ph.D. Course students came up with her initial intended book title, *Lessons from the Dog Park.* It met the *catchy* criteria, but it will be a book on leadership, and there's no immediate connection. Avoid being too slick to the point your intended reader will skip your book because they don't understand what you're talking about.

One of the books I wrote, and is my favorite to this day, *Business Dating: Applying Relationship Rules in Business for Ultimate Success,* has never gained the traction I'd hoped it would. Several (and my heart breaks to write this), *many more than I would ever like,* people have told me they thought this book was about "dating at work." It's about networking and business development. In my quick-witted way, I missed the mark. It's on my list to re-title and update, but darn, have I missed many an opportunity!

## CONNECTED

**Connect something positive with your message.** Hal also connected a period of time when people usually struggle, obviously the morning, and combined it with having a miracle. Immediately brains go "HUH?!" and the first question is, *how am I going to have a miracle in the morning when that's the one time of day I really struggle?*

By connecting something people want (a miracle) with a period of conflict (the morning), he's created the opportunity for discoverability for his book and his formula. He's also made it incredibly easy for people to remember his book.

More on this later.

Crisp. Catchy. Connected. You'll note I used alliteration, which is defined as *using two or more words in a word group that begin with the same letter, such as apt alliteration's artful aid.* Incidentally, Hal also used alliteration in his book title. He gets three gold stars for crafting his title and being crisp, catchy, and connected. There are more gold stars for him to come, but you and I have a little more work to do on this concept of crafting a title that readers will *remember*.

Those aren't the only three options for making your work something people can recall, even with their brains full of other necessary items. Here are a few more to really help you with your book:

## UNCOMMON

I have an uncommon name. It's not easy to remember, but once you know it, it's hard to forget. Saying it properly presents a separate problem, and that *l'accent aigu* confuses those without previous exposure to the French language.

As an aside, I'm used to people "not quite" remembering my name or not using the accent in correspondence. It's so common, in fact, that it's when I receive an email *with* the accent, that I actually notice.

Your book and its contents can offer an uncommon approach; you could use a common word in a peculiar way, or dare I say a strange perspective. (And I do, I do dare. Quite often, in fact.)

One example is the book, *Atomic Habits* by James Clear. When I think "atomic," I think atomic bomb! Then I want to know what in the world atomic has to do with habits. Atomic is defined as *of, pertaining to, resulting from, or using atoms, atomic energy, or atomic bombs.* This book is definitely a powerful example of this key of the Formula. With over 200 weeks on the bestseller list and over 88,000 reviews (and a 4.8 average star rating to boot!), I'd say Mr. Clear hit the nail on the head.

## UNIQUE

Of course, your book is filled with your unique perspective, because you are unique—one of a kind! Only you have your exact background and upbringing, knowledge, education, experience, relationships, and know-how. This exclusive mix is as individual as your fingerprints—and your book's message will be invaluable to your readers because of it.

Think in terms of multiplication though, not addition. The sum of your parts is a force multiplier; you're not just adding *this* to *that*.

I'm well known for not loving math, but I do love multiplication. In fact, I love it when *one plus one equals three.* You know, when two great things come together and create magic? Hello—like chocolate and peanut butter! Peanut butter and jelly! Like peanut butter and just about anything. Or, like psychology and Feng Shui.

Wait, what?

Several years ago, I started studying to get a Feng Shui Master Certification. (If you don't know about Feng Shui, this is a direct message for you to give it a look.) I met Christy Robinson, who is a medical psychologist *and* a Feng Shui Master. Combining her knowledge of people with her knowledge of energy and yin and yang, she helps people to recognize the reciprocal relationship between their minds and homes to create a peaceful, supported, and unlimited life.

I've combined my knowledge and background in sales and selling, my love of personal and professional development, and (obvi) my obsession with books and reading to create my business.

If you have any mental cloudiness around whether or not you've got what it takes, allow me just to take a moment to encourage you by saying, "You do." Just take a good look at your upbringing, schooling, and resume (and if you need to enroll someone in this exercise for additional validation, *do that*), and you will surely find a half-dozen ways you are unique and can bring that to your message.

## UNUSUAL

How can you bring the unusual, also known as amazing, astonishing, exceptional, or surprising, to your message?

*The Prophet* is one example of a book with an exceptional message. When searching for just the right title to reference here, I discovered that this book has been considered a classic for more than forty years, having been originally published in 1923. In fact, it also has been published and re-published during the past *one hundred years* and has more than a dozen individual listings on Amazon alone.

Perhaps you have a message that moves people—emotionally or into action—that can be included in your book, allowing it to be among the many books that stand the test of time.

## CONTRARY

Want people to really remember your message? Take the unpopular or contrarian opinion. Make them feel good about something they normally feel bad about.

In *The Successful Single Mom* series, I took the position that single moms are not to be pitied.

There's no need to feel sorry for moms who are going solo and doing a great job!

In my mastermind, I focus on growing the business you want, not the one you think you need to have. I advocate for intentional and purposeful growth that provides freedom and financial stability over scaling at all costs while being a stressed-out entrepreneur. I encourage meditation, rest, and vacations over eighty-hour weeks and "sleeping when you're dead."

Sharing a position or philosophy *you know in your bones* works, even in the face of loud, opposing views, will cause your readers to think—and when you think, you remember.

If you've never considered these aspects of content creation before, you're not alone. While writing this book, I've had many conversations with people who ask why they have never heard about this before.

*Now you have.* Your book can gain traction simply because you gave some thought to your reader and how to help them in this unique way.

We are far from done, my friend. There are still two other factors you'll want to include in your work.

# CHAPTER THREE BOOK CLUB DISCUSSION QUESTIONS

1. Meeting Key #2: *Easy to Remember,* in your book or WIP, can be done in several ways. Which is your favorite?
2. Which ones do you think will work best for your content?
3. Do you think the concept of helping your reader to remember your content will actually help them remember it?
4. Do you have resistance to this key?
5. What is your biggest takeaway from this chapter?

CHAPTER FOUR

# KEY #3: EASY TO DO

I hope we're good so far and you're excited to help people easily read your content. By now, I bet you're pretty sure they're going to remember it because you've crafted the best possible title and content.

Next, you want your readers to be able to act upon your expertise. It's important that they will be able to put your formula into practice.

I mean, one of the main reasons you're taking the time to write a book is so others can put your advice into practice, isn't it?

That's why I've written this book—so you can replicate what the most successful authors have done to have incredible success with their books *with yours.*

Ensuring readers can *do* what you're sharing can accelerate their success—and when people are successful, what do they do?

They *share*.

But hold on, sharing is the next chapter.

Let's bake something in your book so your readers' success is all but assured. (I mean, you can't do it for them, but you can provide what they need.)

## ENTER: THE FORMULA

Key #3 is to include a formula. Every single one of the books I analyzed to identify *The Bestselling Book Formula* has its own formula, in one fashion or another.

It provides a process—direct, and distinct advice readers can apply to their life, their relationship, or their day (hello again, Miracle Morning), so they can get their desired result.

**Acronyms.** It can come in the form of an acronym, a word formed from the initial letters in each word. The Life SAVERS from *The Miracle Morning* is an example.

This acronym, SAVERS, stands for *silence (meditation), affirmations, visualization, exercise, reading,* and *scribing (journaling).*

When using an acronym, there are a few things to remember:

- Spell out what the acronym stands for when you first introduce it. SAVERS: Silence, Affirmations, Visualization, Exercise, Reading, and Scribing.

- Acronyms are usually written all uppercase. Examples: AWOL, ROFL

- If the acronym has more than four letters and is pronounceable, you can even use upper and lowercase letters. The SAVERS could be written as Savers (this is the author's choice).

- Some acronyms become so familiar you can assume readers know them. *It's a fantastic idea to use a word that can become part of our everyday vernacular.*

**Process.** Perhaps you have a process. In my book, *Vision to Reality,* I provide an overview of the STMA 100-Day Program. STMA is short for Short Term Massive Action. I recently read *The 21 Day Miracle* by Ed Rush. He shares a cool process for accelerated results his readers can apply to almost any area where they'd like to get faster-than-normal results.

In every one of my nonfiction books, I share a process. I've found these elements are helpful and (as of this writing), I plan to expand on them in an upcoming book, *Write Your First Nonfiction Book*, in which a brief synopsis of the contents of this book will be included:

- Chapter One: Encouragement (your reader can create their desired results)
- Chapter Two: Stories and examples
- Chapter Three: An overview of the process
- Chapter Four: Short formula in the form of an acronym, process, or through the use of alliteration; include an overview
- Chapter Five: The Formula-in-action
- Chapter Six: Other tips, tools, resources, and ideas
- Chapter Seven: How to get results in the best possible way
- Chapter Eight: Call-to-Action

I have yet to use an acronym or alliteration in one of my individual books, and that is simply because there hasn't been a logical opportunity to do so.

**Alliteration.** Use a set of words that all start with the same letter. Dan Cumberland, in his upcoming book, title to be determined, uses alliteration by sharing his four P's: People, Process, Product, and Profit.

Whichever one you use, do your best to simplify both your chosen delivery method as well as the information you're sharing with your reader.

If Hal had used *J* for journaling instead of *S* for scribing, he wouldn't have had the whole word. (Sometimes consulting the Thesaurus is a fantastic idea!)

When you can use an acronym, share a process, or apply alliteration and it makes good sense, I say go for it! You could even use *all three of them* in your book if you want (it's your book, right?!). Combined beautifully or used individually, they can assist your reader in reading, remembering, doing, *and* sharing your book.

## CONVEY CONFIDENCE, INCLUDING DETAILS

Once you've shared your expertise with your chosen method (an acronym, process, or using alliteration), go deep.

Give detailed instructions with this two-sided goal in mind: make it *easy* for your reader to be successful—and *hard* (almost impossible!) for them to fail.

In *Go for No!*, Richard Fenton and Andrea Waltz astutely make a case for why getting nos in pursuit of a goal is a superior focus. Then they give a directive: figure out how many nos you usually get to get a yes. *Insert math.* (Hi, still not a math person!) The result is the number of nos you need to get.

Well, I can do simple math. If, to find one hundred readers, I need to ask two hundred readers to read my book, I'm supposed to focus on getting one hundred nos.

(The good news is, after a while, you become immune to the no and get a yes much more often as your skills and confidence increase.)

With the STMA, I helped folks focus on just three goals: two for business, one personal, for one hundred days. They can remember their three goals, they can remember one hundred days, and they can *do it*: it being focus for one hundred days and achieve their three goals.

It helps the reader if you're willing to be vulnerable and authentic and share everything they need to know. You're human, and on the way to discovering what works, you probably ended up with a few cuts and scrapes they would definitely want to avoid. By sharing your experience, they can use your hindsight as their foresight.

A note on sharing personal or sensitive information; share your struggles because it is in the struggles others have faced and triumphed over that we find our own courage to persevere. However, there is such a thing as *too much information* (hint: that's why it is its own acronym: TMI!). If you tend to overshare, keep in mind, there's a line. Here's the question I ask myself; if it were on the cover of *The New York Times* or on a sign in my front yard, would I be embarrassed or regret sharing? If the answer is yes, I reign it in. You can share your experience without making your reader blush or disturbed at a deep level.

Just like a great recipe, which provides both ingredients and detailed instructions for how to use them, a bestselling book needs to be a great recipe.

Include *what they need, how to use it,* and *anything else they need to duplicate your results.* Bonus points if they get better results than you do!

## BUT WHAT IF ...

What if you're providing complex or extremely detailed information for your reader? What if it won't come down to five minutes of this or twenty minutes of that?

You make a good point, and I thought about this, too.

I want to talk for a moment about one of the bestselling books in recent history, *The 4-Hour Work Week* by Tim Ferriss. I mean, if you haven't heard of this book yet, I'd be gob smacked.

It isn't that Tim's philosophy and process is simple or easy. The brilliance of Tim's content is in his title. In fact, the book is huge and chock full of rich, usable, and inspiring information. (I'm going to talk more about this in Chapter Seven.)

There's simply no way any reader will be able to share what's contained in it with a simple acronym or a few words starting with the same letter.

What they will be able to do is remember it and remember to reference it so they can do it.

I worked with Matt Feret to publish *Prepare for Medicare*. If you're outside of the US, Medicare is a program for folks over the age of 65. While all of the details can't be shared here, if you (a) sign up for the wrong plan, (b) sign up at the wrong time, or (c) don't sign up, it's bad news all around. What we wanted was a book title that was easy to remember so readers could *do* what he recommends.

Sometimes, depending upon your content, in order to get readers to *do* what you teach, the one thing they really need to do is get your book!

Ultimately, your readers are looking to you for what they need to do to be successful. They have a problem, and they think the contents of your book can aid them in fixing or eliminating it. Or, you're the expert at creating their desired results, and they want those same (or even better) results. By providing step-by-step instructions, they will be able to eliminate their pain or produce their desired outcome.

Don't make them guess, give as much as you can (within reason). Don't hold back, inasmuch as a book can only contain so much information without a conversation about someone's individual situation. Don't lament the fact that you're sharing everything for less than twenty bucks—your sharing, to the ideal reader—could result in even more business for you. But that's another book!*

Now that you've considered how to help your reader effectively *read* your book, *remember* your title, content, or process, and written it all in a way they feel empowered to *do* it, you've successfully set everything up so that your reader will *share* your book with their world. Let's dive into that aspect of *The Bestselling Book Formula,* so you can become a best earning author.

*One of the reasons I produce courses is because sometimes the best way I can help someone is through the blended learning opportunity courses provide (including live Q&A sessions). You will want to read Lucas Marino's *Monetize Your Book with a Course* to really understand not only how to expand on your book in a course format, but also the huge benefits to your business for doing so.

## CHAPTER FOUR BOOK CLUB DISCUSSION QUESTIONS

1. I've found Key #3: *Easy to Do* has been pivotal to the success of my best earning books. Do you think this could be the same for yours?
2. How can you simplify your process so readers can replicate it in their own lives or businesses?
3. Which route will you take in your book: process, acronym, or using alliteration?
4. Do you have resistance to this key?
5. What is your biggest takeaway from this chapter?

CHAPTER FIVE

# KEY #4: EASY TO SHARE

The number one way new readers discover a book is through personal recommendation. Key #4 is making your book *easy to share.* By ensuring your book is shareable in "all the ways," more of which I cover in this chapter, you're providing the perfect environment for your book to reach outside of your ring of influence.

Let me explain.

I referenced my book *Business Dating* in Chapter Three. That book initially sold pretty well but only because I had a fairly good understanding of how to launch a book and had a decent-sized platform at the time.

The people who have read it, love it. Despite my titling failure, the book has 64 reviews with an average of 4.6/5. The book ranks an abysmal #713,725 in the Amazon Kindle store, which means I haven't sold one in quite a while, probably not in the past several months.

What I intended for this book—to help people engage in effective business networking, so they could flourish in their careers, while avoiding common mistakes—has not come to pass. And while there's a formula included in the book, my 12x12 System™, there just hasn't been enough momentum to keep it going.

All of this to say a few things:

- I've been there. I've made all of the mistakes in at least one of my books, and I hope you will avoid them.
- Your book might be fantastic. But if you fail to do everything in your power to make it *easy to read, remember,* and *do*, you'll greatly limit the possibility it is *easy to share.*
- I want you to be successful. Thus, I've written this book.

## EASY TO SHARE FTW!

For the win, make your book *easy to share.*

When you adhere to *The Bestselling Book Formula,* you've done the pre-work to set the stage for easy sharing on the part of your readers. But let's circle back to the idea of not leaving this important piece to chance. Just because you've got a readable book readers can remember and replicate does not mean they'll automatically share it. They will probably need some encouragement. Even as your readers will appreciate the "do this, don't do that" included in your formula, they won't mind if you also ask, "If you enjoyed my book and benefitted from it, would you please share it?"

In addition to including *read, remember,* and *do,* you can include some gentle asks and instructions to encourage readers to share. Your ask needs to be direct and unrelated to your acronym, process, or in the form of alliteration.

What people want is your recipe—exactly what you've done to be successful and avoid failure, step-by-step. Solve their problem and help them avoid pain and suffering, and they won't mind doing a little something for their new favorite author! The truth is it won't hurt to include an ask to share your book with others.

If you'll indulge me, I'm going to use this book as an example.

- I've chosen to share my formula for writing a best earning book in this book, including sharing the difference between bestselling (which is what you probably thought you wanted when you bought this book) and best earning (which is what I think all authors truly want).
- I used words that are important to aspiring bestselling authors in the title: *bestselling* and *book* and even *formula*.
- I've kept it simple, short, and straightforward. I've done everything in this book I'm suggesting you do in yours.

Using the principle of "where there is one, there are many" (usually used to describe a pest problem), I know writers and aspiring authors find each other and hang out together. They listen to podcasts where successful writers talk about what they do (i.e., *share their formula for success*), do NaNoWriMo (National Novel Writing Month) in November, and join book clubs and writing groups.

It is my intention you will find relief and inspiration inside the pages of this book, and not only apply what you've learned to your book, but you'll do a few of other things as well.

1. You'll look at the books on your desk and shelves while applying *The Bestselling Book Formula* and realize why some have done better than others.
2. You'll read the entire book (honest, 5-star reviews are also most welcome).
3. You'll enthusiastically share it with other writers and authors you know.
4. You might have a bestselling book and encourage aspiring authors to read this one when they ask how you did it.

I had a lovely conversation with J. T. Ellison (world-renowned thriller writer) recently, and she shared that Cal Newport, on his awesome podcast, Deep Questions with Cal Newport, tried to drill her down on "how she does it" (write incredible books, book after book) and her response was, in part, "It's art! It's art!" While that's so very true, much of writing and creating is, indeed, art; success leaves clues, and formulas are made up of clues.

With this formula, I intend for your book to become a best earning book for you because you've added the art aspect to it. And because of that, you add it to the list of books you recommend to other writers and authors.

How specifically, you ask? Again, kindly indulge me with the following list, which you can *also* apply to your book. (I actually share a very similar list to this one in Chapter Eight, customized to you and your book.)

- Write your review and share it. *Include a page in your book's back matter asking readers to, if they enjoyed the book and found it useful, leave a review online.*
- Post a photo on social media of you holding up your Kindle or physical copy of the book. *Keep a dozen books on hand and every so often, offer to send a signed copy when the recipient tags you on social media in a picture of them with your book.* I'll start: if you're one of the first fifty people to tag me on social media (@honoreecorder on LinkedIn and Facebook, @empirebuilderusa on Instagram) in a picture or video of you with my book, I'll send you a signed copy with a heaping tablespoon of gratitude (US residents only, please).

- When you hear people asking for books to read about the writing process, specifically nonfiction, please add this to your list of recommendations. *As there are dozens of books like your books, and people love book listicles (articles with lists), ask to have your book added to the ones that make sense. Also, why not do an email with a book listicle and include your book?*

- Form a book club of fellow writers or turn your book club into a group of writers—and use this book as your guide. *Why not add discussion questions at the end of each chapter to help your readers along, as I have done in this book.*

- Be sure to grab the book bonuses and tell your author friends about them, too! *Wait, you weren't planning on having book bonuses? Ooh, please don't miss out on this no-brainer way to grow your email list and readership in one fell swoop!* Get the bonuses for this book at HonoreeCorder.com/Formula.

- Buy a few copies of this book and share them. Just yesterday, I was given a book by a friend, *The Book of Mistakes* by Skip Prichard. Incidentally, a personal recommendation is one thing, next level awesome is when someone recommends it while simultaneously giving it as a gift! *Does it make sense for groups or companies to purchase your book in small quantities or large bulk orders? If so, be sure to mention that in your book!*

- When your book becomes a hit, a bestseller that surprises you, even with the great advice included in this book (smile), tell me about it! I want to celebrate your success with you.

By including some or all of the list of suggestions above, you've taken the guesswork out of how your readers can share your book. You're helping them by giving them a path to follow, which I promise they will appreciate! *Don't you appreciate that I'm giving you my formula for a bestselling book?* How you feel is how your readers will feel. Because I receive emails expressing reader appreciation almost every week that include some version of, "Now I know what to do, and I'm more hopeful and less stressed than ever about this!" I've become more encouraged to simply tell readers how to help, because I know they want to.

By sharing what has worked for you, your readers will love you for it, and they will want to engage in the trifecta of awesomeness: help the author (you) by helping a friend, which makes them feel great.

Kind of awesome, right?

Now it's time for me to briefly address the brevity of this book.

## CHAPTER FIVE BOOK CLUB DISCUSSION QUESTIONS

1. Ensuring Key #4: *Easy to Share* is included in your book in multiple ways is a game-changer for authors. How will you encourage readers to share your book?

2. What do you want readers to do to share your book the most?

3. Do you feel comfortable asking people, in this case readers, to help you? If not, how can you begin to feel more comfortable and embrace asking for help?

4. Do you have resistance to this key?

5. What is your biggest takeaway from this chapter?

CHAPTER SIX

# NOT TOO LONG, NOT TOO SHORT, JUUUUST RIGHT!

There seems to be quite a bit of pressure to beef up a book with content—in some cases, more content than is necessary.

You'll note this book is short and sweet; some will be able to read it in less than an hour. *That is my intention.* I don't need to add unnecessary, additional content, so you'll feel like your investment is worthwhile.

I want you to feel like you've been given the golden ticket, the fast pass to writing a bestselling book, without having to trade even one minute more than necessary to learn how to do it.

There's an author I absolutely adore—almost every single one of his books is like drinking a tall glass of ice water on a hot Tennessee day. *Almost.*

There's one book that I'm convinced was the third book in a three-book deal. It covers a simple idea, *over and over and over* for more than three hundred pages. I think it could've been a one-hundred-page book, but I suspect (a) he was paid a lot of money to write it and (b) the directive from the publisher was "It needs to be $x$ number of words and pages. Go!" And go, he did.

I listened to the book on audio, all seven hours of it (the last six hours on double and then triple speed), the whole time waiting for new, interesting, or life-changing distinctions I could apply.

Did it ever come? Nope. I was super annoyed because every other book he's written has been fantastic, every word gold. This book just went over the same, single idea on repeat. I already knew the topic was a good idea; I was looking for some secret sauce. I was after something I didn't already know that I could apply. I never did get it, and I'm still a tiny bit frustrated three years later. LOL

Am I going to tell you who it is? Again, *nope*. That's not my style and not the point of this story.

The point of the story is this; please do not add additional content to your book just to increase your word and page count.

Tell your reader what they need to know; include everything you need to include, nothing more or less. Focus on your reader and their experience—both their reading experience and the one they'll have once they've finished reading and gone on about their life.

You may end up with ten thousand words or eighty thousand words. Whatever is best for your book is best for your book. You want readers to looooooove your book, right? You want them to read it, remember it, do what you teach them, and share it with everyone within the sound of their voice (or fingertips).

Then apply this formula to your book and make sure you keep in mind the amount of time someone will have to trade in order to consume and absorb your wisdom. Do your best to take as little of their time as you can, while giving them the best return on that time investment.

Got it? Good. Then this very short chapter is done!

## CHAPTER SIX BOOK CLUB DISCUSSION QUESTIONS

1. Do you love short books, or do you feel compelled to write more?
2. Do you equate the length of a book to the value the reader receives?
3. Can you let go of the idea *longer is better* and embrace this concept—at least give it a go?
4. Do you have resistance to this idea?
5. What is your biggest takeaway from this chapter?

CHAPTER SEVEN

# BOOKS THAT PASS THE BESTSELLING BOOK FORMULA TEST

If you're wondering if your work-in-progress meets The Bestselling Book Formula Test, or how to make some adjustments, so it does, this chapter can help.

Once you've read it, you'll be able to look at any nonfiction book (and I'm throwing in a fiction book for good measure) and see if it meets the test.

This chapter is dedicated to several books I've read that do pass The Bestselling Book Formula Test with flying colors.

In case you're wondering, I'm not going to analyze books that don't pass; that's not how I roll. What I will do is talk about why the books I've analyzed are doing so well.

Before I dive in, I want to say that this isn't a real test (obviously), and the publishers and authors had no idea they were passing it. While this "test" is of my making, all of these folks are smart people who intelligently and, in some ways, intuitively put their books together.

What's great about knowing this formula is that their book's wild success is now possible for your book, too! You don't have to hope your book will be a massive hit. You can apply the formula and multiply its chances.

These first three books are nonfiction, and I've got one fiction book I put to the test, just to see how it stacks up. You'll have to see for yourself if you agree with my analyses.

In these analyses, I've included some numbers, because I think data is important when defining whether a book is a long-term success. Ranking on Amazon is what I reference here, as well as the number of reviews. It is important to note Amazon's ranking system updates hourly. Also, I know from experience that for every review that's given, there are dozens of books read, and there is no review.

Side note: if you read a book you love, please take some time to leave a review for the book. I thank you on behalf of all authors everywhere.

### *THE MIRACLE MORNING*

I've already talked quite a bit about *The Miracle Morning,* and to recap, here's how it engages the formula:

- **Read.** The writing is simple and straightforward, and it's a fairly fast read.
- **Remember.** The title and the formula are easy to remember. Even remembered "wrong" is still remembered.
- **Do.** The Life SAVERS can be recalled quickly, and Hal even went so far as to give people different options for each of the SAVERS (five minutes for silence, twenty minutes for exercise).
- **Share.** Employing *The Miracle Morning* Life SAVERS is life-changing, and when people are able to change their lives, *they share!* In fact, sometimes people don't have to share—the people around them notice a

change and want to know what in the heck they're doing. Talk about an opportunity!

Before my analysis, I often thought the success of *The Miracle Morning* was a lightning strike—it only happens to one in a million authors. With more years and books of experience under my belt, when I applied the formula to it, I realized it had every box checked (sometimes twice!). The formula, combined with Hal's neverending tenacity and determination to make the book a success, meant there was almost no way it wouldn't be a bestseller!

## THE 4-HOUR WORK WEEK

The next book is *The 4-Hour Work Week: Escape 9-5, Live Anywhere, and Join the New Rich* by Timothy Ferriss. First published in 2007 (sixteen years ago, as of this writing) and an immediate *New York Times Bestseller* published in 35 languages, this book ranks at #1,309 *in hardcover* and #301 in audio with almost 20,000 reviews (average 4.5/5). In other words, it started selling the day it was released, and it is still selling today.

In fact, in 2009, an expanded and revised edition was released. The current edition of the book comes in at a whopping 448 pages and will take over 13 hours of listening time; and is a true bestselling best *earning* book.

What this book does, in addition to getting an A+ on The Bestselling Book Formula Test, is buck any convention that readers "just won't read long books," "won't pay a lot for an ebook," or "won't listen to anything longer than ten minutes."

Listen kids, if you've got content people want, they'll pay any amount of money and spend copious amounts of their time in exchange for it. I digress.

***The 4-Hour Work Week*** engages the formula differently than most others, and here's how:

- **Read.** This isn't a fast read by any stretch; however, it is broken down into easy to identify and compellingly titled sections *that can be read easily and quickly.*

- **Remember.** If, for some reason, you can't remember the DEAL acronym shared in the book (Definition, Elimination, Automation, and Liberation), you'll surely be able to remember the name of the title.

- **Do.** What I remember most about my multiple reads of ***The 4-Hour Work Week*** is (1) it got me excited to create passive income, (2) gave me several strategies and resources *I* could access (they just weren't for the fancy pants author, regular folks could do it, too), and (3) if there was an ~~excuse~~ reason (LOL) I thought I couldn't duplicate Tim's results, he shared tips and hacks to counter my limiting beliefs. He also set reasonable expectations. *If I could do it, dear reader, so can you.*

- **Share.** *The 4-Hour Work Week* changed the lives of those who chose to engage in it; however, what the author shared required time and effort. The book initially got people excited, and that's why they bought the book. But when it helped people leave the jobs they wanted to leave *and* create a life they loved, that's when the fire of sharing started for this book. It hasn't burned out and doesn't look like it ever will.

As with the first book, what at first glance seems like some seriously good luck reveals itself to be part and parcel of exactly what makes a book initially and continuously sell: it's a great book with life-changing content people love to learn about, do, and share.

### *PSYCHO-CYBERNETICS*

The final nonfiction book I tested, *Psycho-Cybernetics: A New Way to Get More Living Out of Life* by Dr. Maxwell Maltz is a unique and interesting bestselling book. My Amazon search yielded at least seven different publication dates of the different volumes. There are two authors (Dan Kennedy and Matt Furey) who have purchased the right to, and have published, their own version of the book as co-authors to Dr. Maltz.

In full transparency, this is one of my favorite books of all time, and I first read it in the early 1990s. I have four of the published versions, the original, with Dan Kennedy, with Matt Furey, and the one I'm sharing about here, *Psycho-Cybernetics Deluxe Edition: The Original Text of the Classic Guide to a New Life.* This version comes in a beautiful hardbound edition with a special cover sleeve. All of the versions are excellent, and it would be hard for me to recommend just one (as you're witnessing here). If you're inclined, I recommend you get and read all of them.

All of this was important to note when considering how beautifully *Psycho-Cybernetics* passes The Bestselling Book Formula Test. The original book was published in 1960, and this newest edition was published in 2016. It has over eighteen hundred ratings on Amazon, 4.7/5 stars, and almost twenty-two *thousand* ratings on Goodreads, 4.2/5, in six years, which is astounding.

*Psycho-Cybernetics* engages the formula differently than most others, and here's how:

- **Read.** This book is also a bit of a tome—at 330 pages, it'll take several hours to read. Although Dr. Maltz was a highly educated man (a plastic surgeon, in fact), the book is simple and easy to read.

- **Remember.** The word *psycho-cybernetics* isn't particularly easy to remember. In fact, one review is titled: ***Funny name. Great book!*** Dr. Maltz explains how these two words come together. The self-image can be enhanced by understanding how to combine psychology and science. More simply, if you want to have a great self-image and increase your chances of success, this guide will teach you how to get your brain to do it automatically. You might not remember all of *that,* but you will remember you wanted to be successful, read Dr. Maltz's book, and within a short time, you were rockin' the casbah. Dr. Maltz calls this the "winning feeling," which is, without a doubt, easy to remember.

- **Do.** The best part about what Dr. Maltz teaches in his book is that it doesn't cost anything, it is easy, and anyone can do it. (Intrigued yet?) What he teaches you to do in the book doesn't take a lot of time, either. It is easy to do in spades.
- **Share.** The book is easy to share because it has an interesting name, is life-changing, and others around you are likely to notice you've changed and ask what you've been doing. So, even if you don't initiate the sharing of the book, you'll most likely have ample opportunity.

Now considered a self-help classic, this book is on course to be a bestselling book for the foreseeable future. And although the book was first published in 1960, as of 2008 the book was recommended in the book *50 Self-Help Classics.*

It might be too much for a first-time (or even fiftieth time) author to think as big as to want a book that is, in future decades, considered one of the best books of all time and continuously recommended. *However,* it makes sense to me to at least attempt to focus on integrating the four keys in *The Bestselling Book Formula* into your book. I'll discuss that in the next chapter, but first and just for fun, I thought I'd include an analysis of a book that seems to be on everyone's *to-read* list these days.

## *VERITY*

*Verity* by Colleen Hoover (who as of this writing, has *the top three* books on Amazon) is an incredible read. It was also the first book of Ms. Hoover's I've read, and they are all good. This one in particular has a bit of a controversy about it (the storyline), and the reviews are split. Released just one year ago, it has an eye-popping 183,002 reviews (4.6/5) already and shows no signs of slowing down.

I read the book in one four-hour, don't-bother-me-or-else reading session. It was *unputdownable*. For giggles, I applied my formula to it, and here's what I've come up with:

- **Read.** No shocker here; the writing is just easy. It was easy to read, and I couldn't turn the pages fast enough.

- **Remember.** This isn't a spoiler; *Verity* is the name of the main character. Read something over and over again, and you'll remember it. Also, the premise of the book, storyline, and suspense all come together in a way that makes it next level: unforgettable. You won't just remember it; you can't forget it.

- **Do.** There's nothing to do with fiction except read it—you want to read it (fast!), and you'll tell everyone you know to "do that, too." There's something about it that had me telling people to move it up in the pile and read it, if not right now, at least next.

- **Share.** All of this combined has made sharing a natural piece. You read it; it's awesome, and you share it. I've now had several conversations that start with, "Have you heard of Colleen Hoover? *Have you read* Verity!?!"

There are several other fiction titles that come to mind that hit the notes I've shared in this book just right: any of the *Harry Potter* series, *Behind Closed Doors* by BA Paris, and any book by Sidney Sheldon, just to name a few. While I haven't read *Where the Crawdads Sing,* no less than two dozen people have been after me to "Read it already!"

I know you're reading this book probably because you want your very own bestselling book, one that truly does make you a fortune. I'm ready when you are!

# CHAPTER SEVEN BOOK CLUB DISCUSSION QUESTIONS

1. Now that you've seen how The Bestselling Book Formula can be applied to almost any book, how excited are you to apply it to yours?
2. Which book featured in this chapter is your favorite example?
3. Which one gives you the most hope your book will be a best earning book?
4. Do you have resistance to this idea?
5. What is your biggest takeaway from this chapter?

CHAPTER EIGHT

# PUT THE BESTSELLING BOOK FORMULA TO WORK IN YOUR BOOK

Now that you know *what* the formula is, and you have the *how,* you can apply it to your book.

We can agree, can't we, it's a great idea to give your book the best chance it can possibly have to make an impact on the world, and in the process, an income for you.

The obvious best time to apply these keys is when you've got an idea, maybe even the first draft of an outline. *However*.

Even if you've already written most of your book and you don't yet have a crystal-clear process, acronym, or know how to apply alliteration, you can make simple adjustments to create extraordinary results.

The important thing to remember here is that you want to include each of the Four Keys as much as you possibly can, in every way you can. I want you to have the bestselling book that's the best earning book your great-grandchildren are *super happy* you wrote!

### KEY #1: MAKE IT EASY TO READ.

Regardless of your subject matter, save a book on performing neurosurgery or calculating formulas for putting rockets in space, you can simplify your writing such that almost anyone can read it. And you should.

We've all read dense text that not only didn't grab us right away, but it was also easy to put down (and thus, never finish). *Make sure your book is easy to read.* The reader will read it, feel great about it, and the rest will be history.

I do remember my high school boyfriend, when talking about a mutual friend, said, "He's just so condescending." And, of course, I nodded my head and said, "Oh, yeah, so condescending." Then I had to go look up the word *in the dictionary* (because it was 1986, okay?). The synonyms provided were *arrogant* and *snooty*. He wasn't wrong (our mutual friend was totally arrogant), but in order to not appear stupid, I nodded my head, verbally agreed, and felt stupid. Please make your readers feel smart-er because they can easily read your book. Cool?

Let me make it easy for you to make your book easy to read:

- Again, I suggest you go ahead and write with abandon. Let the words flow freely! I write like I talk. Sometimes that's good, other times not so much.

- Be conversational in your tone, straightforward in your advice, and if it is your personality, be fun!

- Then, go through and give a second look at any ~~esoteric~~ complex words and do what I did just now: cross them out and use a basic word in its place.

- Next, and you're going to love this tool, go to Renaissance.com, then use the dropdown menu under Resources to find the ATOS Analyzer. At the bottom of that page, you can "Analyze a book." Click that button and then upload your manuscript. It will give you a report, including the following:

- ATOS Book Level. This book is 6.8, and you'll recall it is suggested to write at or below the 7th grade level.
- Average Word Length. This book's average word length is 4.4, meeting the "shorter words are better" suggestion.
- Average Sentence Length. This book's average sentence length, before editing, is a whopping sixteen words. Oops. Well, nobody's perfect. (But hold on, we're not done yet.)

- Then you'll make a note of where you are. Still too many "big" words? Make some swaps. Grade level too high? More changes might be necessary. Long sentences? Cut those suckers in half. Use more periods and fewer conjunctions.
- Finally, ask your editorial team (editor(s) and proofreaders) for help. Tell them what you're trying to do and ask them to make suggestions or call out places where you can say more with less, in a simpler way.

A final note for you overthinkers (hi, I totally see you!): *don't*. You don't need to replace every "preference" with "rank." Sometimes a longer, more complex word *is the right word*. Sometimes a longer sentence is required. It won't be the end of the world if a reader has to look up a word. They will learn something else in the process of reading your book. In my book, that's a bonus.

## KEY #2: MAKE IT EASY TO REMEMBER.

Next, let's make your book memorable, as in *easy to remember*.

- **Keep your title and/or formula as simple and memorable as humanly possible.**

  - **No further explanation can be necessary.** You won't be there to explain how "it's not how to date in the office—it's a book about networking!" Someone, anyone, and everyone needs to *get it* right off the bat. Within a microsecond, your prospective reader will become a reader or not.

  - **Don't be cute or clever; direct and simple is better.** I know you're smart. Hello, you're writing a book. Duh. So are Hal, Tim, Maxwell, and Colleen.

- **Short and sweet FTW.** Be as blunt, short, and concise as you dare, while still maintaining your voice, making the point, and expressing your personality.

- **Use an acronym or word (HALT!) that can be recalled fairly easily.**
- **Keep the words the acronym is made of *also* simple and easy to recall.**
- **If you use alliteration, use the least number of actual words possible.** Three Ps is better than the 72 ways to…

The ability to recall your process, acronym, or alliterative words just after you publish is fine, but the ability to recall it or them years later is really the test. If you, the author, won't be able to recall them years later, chances are your reader won't be able to, either. Please keep working on it until it's so good and simple, you'll never be able to forget; this will help your readers immensely.

## KEY #3: MAKE IT EASY TO DO.

Let's circle back to Hal Elrod and *The Miracle Morning*. If you don't know the story, Hal went in search of the practices the most successful people used to be, well, successful. He identified them: meditation, affirmations, visualization, reading, exercising, and journaling. You'll note that if he'd tried to make an acronym out of those words, it would be MAVREJ. Well, that's not a word. It is *gibberish*. So, he consulted a thesaurus, turning *meditation* into *silence* and *journaling* into *scribing*. *Voilà !* Now we have a word: SAVERS— and the Life SAVERS was born.

Next, he knew that doing all of them every day would be helpful, so he assigned time to each practice. Five minutes each for four of them and twenty minutes each for two of them. Now we have the recipe for success: one hour total plus six practices, initially for thirty days, equals quantum leap.

For the nerds in the group, here's your formula:

One hour + six practices ~ thirty days = quantum leap!

You have your own recipe; share it in a way your readers can do it with the least amount of effort, for the shortest amount of time to see results, while feeling successful and good about it.

Here are a few ways:

- **Keep "one-two-three-too-many" in mind.** The brain can easily remember three items. Example: *Write down your goals. Review them twice a day. Say a positive affirmation* *for each one.* Recall becomes exponentially more difficult with each step or piece added after three. The SAVERS helps because it's a word, and it is a word that makes sense.

- **Take out any guesswork.** When it is time for your reader to *do* what you advise, they need to know exactly *what* to do, *when* to do it, for *how long*, and *in what order*. Be exact. Be specific. Give good, simple directions. "Determine your target publishing date. Decide how much time you have to devote to writing your book. Schedule at least fifteen minutes to write every day." Tell what you think they will need to know to be successful, then share a little bit more. Remember; they aren't inside your brain, and you won't be there to close any open loops.

- **Make it fast and easy, when possible.** Assuming your book isn't an instruction manual for training for an Ironman, you can give examples and insight into how your reader can replicate your results with the least amount of time and effort (and even money) possible.

When your readers can duplicate your results—or achieve even better ones for themselves, they will feel satisfied and successful. It is the goal, and it is magical when it happens and they tell you about it! (When that happens, you're going to be so thrilled.)

## KEY #4: MAKE IT EASY TO SHARE.

When you meet the first three criteria of this formula, chances are you will have automatically engaged, at least to some degree, word of mouth.

I know you'll want to give a nudge to readers, so they'll intentionally share your book, too.

To that end, there are some additional requests you can make of your reader. Those who have been successful with your book's content may do one or two—and that will be amazing! A few blessed souls will do all of them (some people are awesome like that).

You might recognize this list from Chapter Five, now tailored to you and your book:

- Ask readers to write a review and share it. *Include a page in your book's back matter asking readers to, if they enjoyed the book and found it useful, leave a review online.*

- On your social media, ask readers to post a photo of your book cover on Kindle or holding a physical copy of the book. *Keep a dozen books on hand and every so often, offer to send a signed copy when they tag you on social media in a picture of them with your book.*

- Create a listicle (a list of books similar to yours) recommending books like your book—and be sure to include yours. Be sure to tag the other authors and send them the email you shared with your list. Author friends are the best.

- Suggest readers include your book in their book club or form a new book club. Why not add discussion questions at the end of each chapter to help your readers along, as I have done in this book.

- Create some valuable bonuses to go along with the book and remind readers to be sure to get them. You won't want to miss out on this no-brainer way to grow your email list and readership in one fell swoop! Get this book's bonuses at [HonoreeCorder.com/Formula](HonoreeCorder.com/Formula).

- If it works for your type of book, have a page on your website where you sell books in bulk. On my website, I offer the opportunity for fans of *The Miracle Morning for Teachers* and *The Miracle Morning Art of Affirmations Coloring Book* to sponsor a classroom by buying two copies of the book for teachers and thirty coloring books for students. I also include access to a course I created for teachers about how to personally use the Life SAVERS as well as share them in their classrooms. You can find more info at HonoreeCorder.com/miraclemorning.

- Ask readers to send you an email if they've read your book and loved it. Those emails are my very favorite, and I know you'll love them, too!

If you have any reservations about asking your readers to share about your book, and you want to rely on hope, I am going to remind you that *hope is not a strategy.* The four authors I talk about in this book did not just hope readers would share their books—they also host and/or are guests on podcasts, send email newsletters, do public speaking or public appearances, or both. As they pray, they move their feet. So should you.

While book marketing is what I'm referencing here, that is another book. (Literally, I wrote a book about book marketing: *You Must Market Your Book.*) In addition to setting your book up for success by engaging the four keys in it, you'll want to educate yourself on how to market your book. Overnight, magical stories of authors who just published their book and then raked in piles of cash do happen, but darn it if most of us have to work at it.

Do everything in this book that makes sense for you, and also plan to work at it.

## KEEP IT AS SHORT AS HUMANLY POSSIBLE.

This book is right around 15,000 words and shares just four keys in The Bestselling Book Formula.

I'm sure I could've added more examples and stories and made up other keys to have a longer book, and you probably would have read it. Believe me, if there were more words needed, I would have included them. If there was a fifth key, or I would've discovered seventy-seven keys, I would have written about them.

I didn't. There weren't.

Write what needs to be written, not a word more or less. There's no right or wrong length of a book; only include what is needed.

I often hear readers say they prefer short books that get to the point (and they certainly don't mind longer books, when they don't feel the extra time spent reading is a waste). I'm curious to know where you sit on the subject. Feel free to shoot me an email at Honoree@HonoreeCorder.com. I'd love to hear from you.

Before I go, I have one more important thought.

## BE YOURSELF. EVERYONE ELSE IS ALREADY TAKEN.

As part of my analysis, I couldn't help but note that all four of these authors—three nonfiction and one fiction—all march to the beat of their own drum.

While there are standards authors must meet with their books and hoops they must jump through to become bestsellers (I've included four of them in this book), each of these authors brings their unique voices and authenticity to the table.

I don't want to neglect this point. While getting advice about your writing and your book, including from me, can be helpful as you pursue writing your own bestselling book, you'll experience your most incredible success when you do what makes the most sense *to you*.

Finding and sharing your unique voice from your unique perspective in your chosen way, is one of the ingredients in a long-term, bestselling, and best earning book.

Take every piece of advice and insight you get and analyze it for what it's worth. Decide what *you* think about it and whether it applies to you. Then listen to your gut and do what you think is best.

## THE END IS JUST THE BEGINNING

Now you have a book to write (or finish writing). I've given you everything I've got, and I know it can help you. Please be sure to grab the bonuses I've included with this book (HonoreeCorder.com/Formula) and shoot me an email sometime and let me know how it's going.

# **AUTHOR'S NOTES**

Thank you for reading this book! It is the direct result of a conversation I had with Kent Sanders about a newsletter I had written of the same title.

Because he's in my Empire Builders Mastermind, he scheduled a chat just to go over this formula. Kent wondered why he hadn't ever heard about this before, and I said because it wasn't something I'd heard, it was something I'd discovered—made up, if you will—throughout my years of publishing books.

All things being equal, I have always wondered why some books do better than others. Even when there's a "lightning strike" (a book does so well, it is almost inexplicable), I have wondered what was really behind the curtain. In my quest to find out, I identified the four keys I shared in this book.

Kent suggested I turn it into a book, and so I did.

I wrote the book during my early morning writing time, overlooking my yard, throughout the fall of 2022. This time of year, the sun comes up as I'm writing, and it's fun to take a break to refill my coffee cup and marvel at the colors in the sky. They are breathtaking, and sometimes I post a photo on my Instagram (which, of course, does not do it justice).

I had a lot of time to reflect more deeply about why some books, those that are simply amazing, didn't really make an impact. Yet, others had incredible staying power, even without being particularly well published.

Some are fast-paced, easy reads, chock full of great information—but the title was off, there was no formula, and I didn't leave with more than a good feeling. Others had a formula, but I couldn't commit three hours a day. Still, others were great, but when I tried to recall the author's name or *anything* about the title, I was stumped. In each instance, the moment to share passed for me, as I'm sure it did for others.

I decided Kent was right—and because I want to help authors succeed (big!), I got to work.

My initial findings jelled even more as I picked up random books on my shelf and analyzed their commercial performance through the lens of my formula.

Because I think I've figured out something cool that is also valuable, I was excited to rise each morning before the sun to share this with you. So even though we may not know each other, I hope what I've discovered will help you not only write your book. I hope it will help you craft it in a way that helps you to reach more readers, sell more books, and make more money.

For those of you who have already published and wish you'd discovered this formula sooner, here are a few ideas:

- If you self-published, consider publishing a second edition.

- Just as I have *The Bestselling Book Formula Action Guide* to accompany this book, designed to help you write your bestselling book, adding a workbook (companion guide, planner, or journal) can provide added benefit to your readership.

- Because you know so much more than you can possibly put in a book, you might want to start a podcast related to the book. If you already have a podcast, do a series based on your book.

- A membership community, like the one hosted by Kent Sanders (The Daily Writer Club) can help people take action on the book's ideas, as can a coaching program (like my STMA 100-Day Coaching Program, as covered in my book, *Vision to Reality*).
- Host a page on your website dedicated to your book and offer a free lead magnet or download that expands on the book's main idea. It can give people practical ways to DO and SHARE those ideas.

It was my intention to write a book that helps you write a bestselling and best earning book—one that makes an impact in the world and a fortune for you. When you do, please be sure to reach out and say hello.

Honorée Corder
November 2022

# PUT THE BESTSELLING BOOK FORMULA TO WORK IN YOUR BOOK!

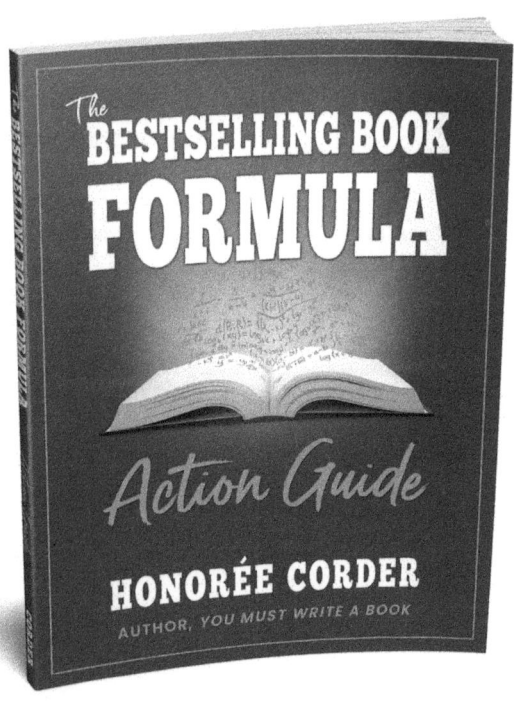

Grab *The Bestselling Book Formula Action Guide* at [HonoreeCorder.com/ActionGuide](HonoreeCorder.com/ActionGuide)

# BESTSELLING BOOK FORMULA MINI-COURSE

If you want more, check out the mini-course I've created, with the same title as this book, to ensure your book will be a best *earning* book for many years to come.

Learn more at
<u>HonoreeCorder.com/BSBFCourse</u>

# BOOK RECOMMENDATIONS

One of the very early readers of this book asked me to name all of my books for writers, so here they are:

- *You Must Write a Book: Boost Your Brand, Get More Business, and Become the Go-To Expert*

- *You Must Market Your Book: Increase Your Impact, Sell More Books, and Make More Money*

- The Prosperous Writer Book Series: *Prosperity for Writers: A Writer's Guide to Creating Abundance; The Nifty 15: Write Your Book in 15 Minutes a Day; The Prosperous Writer's Guide to Making More Money; The Prosperous Writer's Guide to Finding Readers; The Prosperous Writer's Productivity Journal.* Three of these are with Brian D. Meeks.

- The Like a Boss Book Series: *Write Like a Boss; Publish Like a Boss, Market like a Boss.* All with Ben Hale.

- *The Miracle Morning for Writers* with Hal Elrod and Steve Scott

Be sure to check out my favorite book recommendations for writers at HonoreeCorder.com/myfavoritebooks.

# WOULD YOU KINDLY REVIEW THIS BOOK?

If you've enjoyed this book, please take just two minutes to leave a review where you bought it (and maybe even on Goodreads.com)? I'd be eternally grateful! Thank you!

# **GRATITUDE**

A mighty big thank you goes to Kent Sanders—for his suggestion that I write this book. An extra huge thanks for reading the ugly first draft and giving me a couple of value pointers. When he said, "I wish this was a book!" I added it to my production schedule. Only another author knows what it means to suggest writing an entire book. From one writer to another, you're the bee's knees.

To my husband, partner, and best friend, Byron—I don't know what I did before you came into my life, but it sure has been extra wonderful since you did. I give a shit, honey.

To my BFF, Renee, thank you for being my levity, support, and "all the things." I know, you know.

Karen Hunsanger, my editor-plus! You made crazy good suggestions, and helped me enhance it. You're the best, cookie!

Terry Stafford, my proofreader extraordinaire. Thanks so much for putting the final polish on this book.

Dino—you rock, as always! Your design genius blesses all of my books, and you're incomparable. Thank you.

# WHO IS HONORÉE CORDER?

Honorée Corder is an empire builder with more than a dozen six- and seven-figure income streams. She's an executive and strategic book coach, a TEDx speaker, and an author of more than 50 books (including *You Must Write a Book*) with over four million books sold worldwide. Honorée passionately mentors aspiring empire builders, coaching them to write, publish and monetize their books, create a platform, and develop multiple streams of income. Find out more at HonoreeCorder.com.

Honorée Enterprises Publishing, LLC
Honoree@HonoreeCorder.com
HonoreeCorder.com
https://www.linkedin.com/in/honoree/
Twitter: @honoree
Instagram: @empirebuilderusa
Facebook: https://www.facebook.com/Honoree

www.ingramcontent.com/pod-product-compliance
Lightning Source LLC
Chambersburg PA
CBHW041325110526
44592CB00021B/2832